German Short Stories for Beginners for Beginners Book 1

Over 100 Dialogues and Daily Used Phrases to Learn German in Your Car. Have Fun & Grow Your Vocabulary, with Crazy Effective Language Learning Lessons

www.LearnLikeNatives.com

TABLE OF CONTENT

INTRODUCTION

Before we dive into some German, I want to congratulate you, whether you're just beginning, continuing, or resuming your language learning journey. Here at Learn Like a Native, we understand the determination it takes to pick up a new language and after reading this book, you'll be another step closer to achieving your language goals.

As a thank you for learning with us, we are giving you free access to our 'Speak Like a Native' eBook. It's packed full of practical advice and insider tips on how to make language learning quick, easy, and most importantly, enjoyable. Head over to LearnLikeNatives.com to access your free guide and peruse our huge selection of language learning resources.

5

Learning a new language is a bit like cooking—you need several different ingredients and the right technique, but the end result is sure to be delicious. We created this book of short stories for learning German because language is alive. Language is about the senses—hearing, tasting the words on your tongue, and touching another culture up close. Learning a language in a classroom is a fine place to start, but it's not a complete introduction to a language.

In this book, you'll find a language come to life. These short stories are miniature immersions into the German language, at a level that is perfect for beginners. This book is not a lecture on grammar. It's not an endless vocabulary list. This book is the closest you can come to a language immersion without leaving the country. In the stories within, you will see people speaking to each other, going through daily life situations, and using the most common, helpful words and phrases in language.

You are holding the key to bringing your German studies to life.

Made for Beginners

We made this book with beginners in mind. You'll find that the language is simple, but not boring. Most of the book is in the present tense, so you will be able to focus on dialogues, root verbs, and understand and find patterns in subject-verb agreement.

This is not "just" a translated book. While reading novels and short stories translated into German is a wonderful thing, beginners (and even novices) often run into difficulty. Literary licenses and complex sentence structure can make reading in your second language truly difficult—not to mention BORING. That's why German Short Stories for Beginners is the perfect book to pick up. The stories are simple, but not infantile. They were not written for children, but the language is simple so that beginners can pick it up.

The Benefits of Learning a Second Language

If you have picked up this book, it's likely that you are already aware of the many benefits of learning a second language. Besides just being fun, knowing more than one language opens up a whole new world to you. You will be able to communicate with a much larger chunk of the world. Opportunities in the workforce will open up, and maybe even your day-to-day work will be improved. Improved communication can also help you expand your business. And from a neurological perspective, learning a second language is like taking your daily vitamins and eating well, for your brain!

How To Use The Book

The chapters of this book all follow the same structure:

- A short story with several dialogs
- A summary in German
- A list of important words and phrases and their English translation
- Questions to test your understanding
- Answers to check if you were right
- The English translation of the story to clear every doubt

You may use this book however is comfortable for you, but we have a few recommendations for getting the most out of the experience. Try these tips and if they work for you, you can use them on every chapter throughout the book.

1) Start by reading the story all the way through. Don't stop or get hung up on any particular words or phrases. See how much of the plot you can understand in this way. We think you'll get a lot more of it than you may expect, but it is completely normal not to understand everything in the story. You are learning a new language, and that takes time.

2) Read the summary in German. See if it matches what you have understood of the plot.

3) Read the story through again, slower this time. See if you can pick up the meaning of any words or phrases you don't understand by using context clues and the information from the summary.

4) Test yourself! Try to answer the five comprehension questions that come at the end of each story. Write your answers

down, and then check them against the answer key. How did you do? If you didn't get them all, no worries!

5) Look over the vocabulary list that accompanies the chapter. Are any of these the words you did not understand? Did you already know the meaning of some of them from your reading?

6) Now go through the story once more. Pay attention this time to the words and phrases you haven't understand. If you'd like, take the time to look them up to expand your meaning of the story. Every time you read over the story, you'll understand more and more.

7) Move on to the next chapter when you are ready.

Read and Listen

The audio version is the best way to experience this book, as you will hear a native German speaker tell you each story. You will become accustomed to their accent as you listen along, a huge plus for when you want to apply your new language skills in the real world.

If this has ignited your language learning passion and you are keen to find out what other resources are available, go to **LearnLikeNatives.com**, where you can access our vast range of free learning materials. Don't know where to begin? An excellent place to start is our 'Speak Like a Native' free eBook, full of practical advice and insider tips on how to make language learning quick, easy, and most importantly, enjoyable.

And remember, small steps add up to great advancements! No moment is better to begin learning than the present.

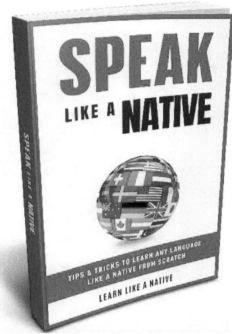

CHAPTER 1
The Mysterious Package /
Greetings

HANDLUNG

Es klingelt an der Tür.

Andrew läuft zur Tür der Wohnung. Die Türklingel klingelt am Samstagmorgen nie. Andrew freut sich, zu sehen, wer an der Tür ist. Er öffnet die Tür.

"**Guten Morgen**, kleiner Junge", sagt ein Bote. Der Mann ist in einer braunen Uniform gekleidet und trägt eine braune Schachtel.

"**Hallo, der Herr**", sagt Andrew.

"Ich habe ein Paket", sagt der Lieferant, "für die Hauptstraße 10."

"Das ist die Hauptstraße 10", sagt Andrew.

"Das Paket hat keinen Namen", sagt der Lieferant, "es hat auch keine Wohnungsnummer."

"Wie seltsam!" sagt Andrew.

"Kannst du es der richtigen Person geben?" fragt der Mann.

"Ich kann es versuchen", sagt Andrew. Er ist erst zehn Jahre alt, aber er fühlt sich wichtig.

"Vielen Dank", sagt der Lieferant. Er geht, Andrew bringt die Schachtel in sein Haus. Er starrt auf die Schachtel. Sie hat ungefähr die Größe eines Schuhkartons. Auf dem Paket steht kein Name, nur Hauptstraße 10.

Andrew öffnet den Pappkarton. Er muss wissen, was drin ist, um den Besitzer zu finden. In dem

Pappkarton befindet sich eine kleine Holzkiste. Andrew öffnet die Holzkiste. In der Kiste sind 10 verschiedene Brillenpaare. Sie haben unterschiedliche Farben: rosa und rot, grüne Pünktchen, schwarz und weiß. Sie haben auch unterschiedliche Formen: rund, quadratisch und rechteckig.

Er schließt die Schachtel und zieht seine Schuhe an.

"Tschüss, Mama! Ich bin gleich wieder da", schreit er.

Andrew klopft an die Tür gegenüber von seiner Wohnung. Sie öffnet sich. Eine sehr alte Dame lächelt Andrew mit seiner Schachtel an.

"Guten Morgen, Frau Smith!" sagt Andrew.

"**Wie geht es dir**?" fragt die alte Dame.

"**Gut, danke! Und Ihnen**?" fragt Andrew.

"Was hast du da?" fragt die alte Dame.

"**Fräulein**, das ist ein Paket. Es gehört jemandem in diesem Gebäude, aber ich weiß nicht wem", sagt Andrew.

"Es ist nicht für mich", sagt die alte Dame. "Unmöglich!"

"Oh, okay" sagt Andrew, enttäuscht. Die alte Dame trägt eine Brille. Er denkt sich, dass die Brillen ihr gut stehen würden. Er dreht sich um, zu gehen.

"Komm später wieder", ruft die alte Dame, "ich mache Kekse und ein paar Kekse sind für dich und deine Familie."

Andrew geht die Treppe hoch. Sein Gebäude hat 2 Etagen. Er ist mit fast jedem im Gebäude befreundet. Allerdings hat die Wohnung im ersten Stock eine neue Familie. Andrew kennt sie nicht. Er ist schüchtern, aber er klingelt. Ein braunhaariger Mann öffnet die Tür, er lächelt.

"**Hallo**!" sagt der Mann.

"Hallo", sagt Andrew, "ich wohne unten, **mein Name ist** Andrew."

"**Schön, dich kennenzulernen**, Andrew", sagt der Mann. "Wir sind neu im Haus, ich bin Herr Jones."

"Freut mich auch, Sie kennenzulernen" sagt Andrew. "Dieses Paket gehört jemandem in diesem Gebäude. Ist es Ihr Paket?"

"Unmöglich!" sagt der Mann. "Meine Familie und ich sind gerade erst hergezogen. Niemand kennt unsere Adresse."

"Okay", sagt Andrew. "Schön, Sie kennen zu lernen." Die Tür schließt sich. Ein weiteres Nein. Es sind nur noch zwei weitere Wohnungen übrig. In der nächsten Wohnung lebt eine Familie. Die Tochter geht auf dieselbe Schule wie Andrew. Sie ist ein Jahr älter als Andrew. Ihr Name ist Diana. Andrew findet sie sehr hübsch, er fühlt sich wieder schüchtern, aber er klopft an die Tür.

Ein hübsches, blondes Mädchen öffnet die Tür.

"**Hallo**, Diana", Andrew lächelt.

"**Was ist los?**" fragt Diana. Ihr Pijama ist hellrosa und ihre Haare sind zerzaust.

"**Wie läuft es denn so?**" fragt Andrew.

"**Es geht so**", sagte Diana. "Ich habe geschlafen, du hast mich geweckt."

"Es tut mir leid", sagt er schnell. Sein Gesicht ist rot. Er fühlt sich besonders schüchtern. "Ich habe ein Paket. Wir wissen nicht, wem es gehört."

"Was ist drin?" fragt Diana.

"Ein paar Gläser. Sie sind zum Lesen da", sagt Andrew.

"Ich trage keine Brille, meine Mutter trägt auch keine, das Paket ist nicht für uns", sagt Diana.

"Okay", sagt Andrew. Er winkt zum Abschied und geht die Treppe hoch. Es gibt noch eine weitere Wohnung, die Wohnung im zweiten Stock. Herr Edwards lebt allein in dieser Wohnung. Er hat einen großen Papagei, der weiß, wie man redet. Er hat auch vier Katzen und einen Hund. Seine Wohnung ist alt und dunkel. Andrew hat Angst vor Herr Edwards. Er klingelt an der Tür. Er muss herausfinden, wem das Paket gehört.

"**Hallo**," sagt Herr Edwards. Sein Hund kommt zur Tür. Der Hund hilft Herr Edwards, da er blind ist.

"Hallo, Herr Edwards. Ich bin es Andrew", sagt Andrew. Herr Edwards hat die Augen geschlossen, er lächelt.

"Was gibt es Neues, Andrew?" fragt er. Hmmm, denkt Andrew, vielleicht ist Herr Edwards nicht furchterregend. Vielleicht ist Herr Edwards nur ein netter alter Mann, der allein lebt.

"Ich habe ein Paket und ich denke, es ist für Sie", sagt Andrew.

"Oh ja! Meine Lesebrillen, endlich!" lächelt Herr Edwards. Er streckt seine Hände aus. Andrew ist verwirrt. Er sieht den Hund an. Er scheint auch zu lächeln. Er gibt Herr Edwards die Schachtel.

"Schön, dich zu sehen", sagt Herr Edwards.

"Sie auch", sagt Andrew. Vielleicht besucht er Herr Edwards wieder an einem anderen Tag. Er dreht sich um und geht nach Hause.

ZUSAMMENFASSUNG

Ein Junge, Andrew, bekommt ein Paket, das nicht für ihn bestimmt ist. Darin enthalten ist eine Schachtel mit Brillen. Er geht damit zu den Nachbarn, einen nach dem anderen, um herauszufinden, wem das Paket gehört. Er findet heraus, dass das Paket seinem Nachbarn Herr Edwards gehört, was ein wenig überraschend ist.

VOKABELLISTE

guten Morgen	Good morning
Hallo	Hello
Herr	Sir
vielen Dank	Thank you very much
Tschüss	Bye
Guten Morgen!	Morning!
Wie geht es dir?	How are you?

In Ordnung, danke schön!	Fine, thanks!
Und was ist mit dir?	And you?
Fräulein	Ma'am
Hallo	Hi
Mein Name ist...	My Name is...
Freut mich, dich kennenzulernen	It's nice to meet you
Freut mich auch, Sie kennenzulernen	Nice to meet you too
Wie läuft es so?	How's it going?
Es geht so	It's going
Hallo	Hey
Wie läuft es denn so	What's up
Was gibt's Neues	What's new
Schön, dich zu sehen	It's good to see you

FRAGEN

1. Wer ist an der Haustür, wenn Andrew sie öffnet?

    a) ein Lieferant

    b) eine Katze

    c) ein Volkszähler

    d) sein Vater

2. Wie würden Sie Frau Smith beschreiben?

    a) ein schönes Mädchen

    b) eine gemeine Person

    c) ein schlechter Nachbar

    d) eine nette alte Frau

3. Wer wohnt im ersten Stock des Wohnhauses?

    a) niemand

b) ein Mädchen aus Andrews Schule

c) eine neue Familie

d) Andrew

4. Was denkt Andrew über Diana?

a) er mag sie und findet sie hübsch

b) er folgt ihr in den sozialen Medien

c) er mag sie nicht

d) sie kennen sich nicht

5. Wem gehören die Brillen im Haus?

a) der alten Frau

b) dem blinden Mann

c) Andrew und seiner Familie

d) niemand

ANTWORTEN

1. Wer ist an der Haustür, wenn Andrew sie öffnet?

a) ein Lieferant

2. Wie würdest du Frau Smith beschreiben?

d) eine nette alte Frau

3. Wer wohnt im ersten Stock des Wohnhauses?

c) eine neue Familie

4. Was denkt Andrew über Diana?

a) er mag sie und findet sie hübsch

5. Wem gehören die Brillen im Haus?

b) dem blinden Mann

Translation of the Story

The Mysterious Package

The doorbell rings.

Andrew runs to the door of the apartment. The doorbell never rings on Saturday mornings. Andrew is excited to see who is at the door. He opens the door.

"**Good morning**, little boy," says a delivery man. The man is dressed in a brown uniform and is carrying a brown box.

"**Hello, sir**," says Andrew.

"I have a package," the delivery man says. "It says 10 Main Street."

"This is 10 Main Street," says Andrew.

"The package has no name," says the delivery man. "It also has no apartment number."

"How strange!" says Andrew.

"Can you give it to the right person?" the man asks.

"I can try," says Andrew. He is only ten years old, but he feels important.

"Thank you very much," says the delivery man. He leaves. Andrew takes the box into his house. He stares at the box. It is about the size of a shoe box. It has no name on the outside, just 10 Main Street.

Andrew opens the cardboard box. He needs to know what is inside to find the owner. There is a small wood box inside the cardboard box. Andrew opens the wooden box. Inside the box are 10 different pairs of eyeglasses. They are different colors: pink and red, green polka dots, black and white. They are also different shapes: round, square and rectangle.

He closes the box and puts on his shoes.

"**Bye** mom! I'll be right back," he shouts.

Andrew knocks on the door across the hall from his house. It opens. A very old lady smiles at Andrew and the box.

"**Morning**, Mrs. Smith!" says Andrew.

"How are you?" asks the old lady.

"Fine, thanks! And you?" says Andrew.

"What do you have?" asks the old lady.

"Ma'am, this is a package. It belongs to someone in this building but I don't know who," says Andrew.

"It's not for me," says the old lady. "Impossible!"

"Oh, ok" says Andrew, disappointed. The old lady wears glasses. He thinks these glasses would look nice on her. He turns to leave.

"Come back later," calls the old lady. "I'm making cookies and some cookies are for you and your family."

Andrew goes up the stairs. His building has three floors. He is friends with almost everyone in the building. However, the apartment on the second floor has a new family. Andrew doesn't know them. He feels shy, but he rings the bell. A brown-haired man opens the door. He smiles.

"Hi!" says the man.

"Hello," says Andrew. "I live downstairs. **My name is** Andrew."

"It's nice to meet you, Andrew," the man says. "We are new to the building. I'm Mr. Jones."

"**Nice to meet you too,**" says Andrew. "This package belongs to someone in this building. Is it your package?"

"Impossible!" says the man. "My family and I just moved here. No one knows our address."

"Ok," says Andrew. "Nice to meet you then." The door closes. Another no. There are only two apartments left to try. In the next apartment is a family. The daughter goes to the same school as Andrew. She is a year older than Andrew. Her name is Diana. Andrew thinks she is very beautiful. He feels shy again, but he knocks on the door.

A pretty, blonde girl opens the door.

"**Hey,** Diana," Andrew smiles.

"What's up?" Diana says. Her pijamas are bright pink and her hair is messy.

"How's it going?" Andrew asks.

"It's going," Diana says. "I was asleep. You woke me up."

"I'm sorry," he says quickly. His face is red. He feels extra shy. "I have a package. We don't know who it belongs to."

"What is in it?" asks Diana.

"Some glasses. They are glasses for reading," says Andrew.

"I don't wear glasses. My mom doesn't use them. The box is not for us," says Diana.

"Ok," says Andrew. He waves goodbye and climbs the stairs. There is one more apartment, the apartment on the third floor. Mr. Edwards lives in this apartment, alone. He has a big parrot that knows how to talk. He also has four cats and a dog. His apartment is old and dark. Andrew feels afraid of Mr. Edwards. He rings the doorbell. He has to find out who the box belongs to.

"Hello," says Mr. Edwards. His dog comes to the door. The dog helps Mr. Edwards because he is blind.

"Hi, Mr. Edwards. It's Andrew," Andrew says. Mr. Edwards has his eyes closed. He smiles.

"What's new, Andrew?" He asks. Hmmm, Andrew thinks, maybe Mr. Edwards isn't scary. Maybe Mr. Edwards is just a nice old man that lives alone.

"I have a package and I think it is for you," says Andrew.

"Ah yes! My reading glasses. Finally!" smiles Mr. Edwards. He holds his hands out. Andrew is confused. He looks at the dog. It seems to be smiling, too. He gives Mr. Edwards the box.

"It's good to see you," says Mr. Edwards.

"You too," says Andrew. Maybe he will visit Mr. Edwards another day. He turns around and goes home.

CHAPTER 2
Mardi Gras / Colors + Days
of the Week

HANDLUNG

Frank tritt aus seiner Haustür. Sein neues Haus ist **violett** mit **blauen** Fenstern. Die Farben sind sehr hell für ein Haus. In New Orleans, seinem neuen Zuhause, sind Gebäude bunt.

Er ist neu in der Nachbarschaft. Frank hat noch keine Freunde. Das Haus neben ihm ist ein großes, **rotes** Gebäude. Eine Familie lebt dort. Frank starrt die Tür an, als ein Mann sie öffnet. Frank grüßt ihn.

"Hallo, Nachbar!" sagt George. Er winkt, Frank geht zum roten Haus.

"Hallo, ich bin Frank, der neue Nachbar", sagt Frank.

"Schön, dich kennenzulernen, mein Name ist George", sagt George. Die Männer schütteln sich die Hände. George hat eine Lichterkette in den Händen. Die Lichter sind **grün**, **lila** und **golden**.

"Wofür sind die Lichter?" fragt Frank.

"Du bist neu", lacht George. "Es ist Mardi Gras, wusstest du das nicht? Diese Farben repräsentieren den Karnevalsfeiertag hier in New Orleans."

"Oh, ja," sagt Frank. Frank weiß nichts über Mardi Gras. Er hat auch keine Freunde, mit denen er Pläne machen kann.

"Heute ist **Freitag**", sagt George. "Es gibt eine Parade namens Endymion. Wirst du mit mir und meiner Familie hingehen und zuschauen?"

"Ja," sagt Frank. "Wunderbar!"

George macht die Lichter an das Haus, Frank hilft George, George macht das Licht an, das Haus sieht festlich aus.

Die Familie und Frank gehen zur Parade. Während des Mardi Gras gibt es in New Orleans jeden Tag Paraden. Die Paraden während der Woche sind klein. Die Paraden am Wochenende, Samstag und Sonntag, sind groß, mit vielen Festwagen und Menschen. Es gibt einen König des Mardi Grases. Sein Name ist Rex.

Mardi Gras bedeutet Faschings**dienstag**. In England heißt es Fastnachtsdienstag. Der Feiertag ist katholisch. Es ist ein Tag vor Ascher**mittwoch**, der Beginn der Fastenzeit. Mardi Gras ist die Feier vor der Fastenzeit, einer ernsten Zeit. Ab **Donnerstag** sind die besonderen Tage vorbei. New Orleans ist berühmt für sein Mardi Gras. Menschen feiern und tragen Masken und Kostüme. Tatsächlich kann man eine

Maske in New Orleans nur zu Mardi Gras tragen. Den Rest des Jahres ist es illegal!

George und seine Familie sehen mit Frank zu, wie die Parade beginnt. Frank ist überrascht. Viele Leute sehen zu, sie stehen im Gras. Festwagen passieren die Gruppe. Festwagen sind große Strukturen mit Menschen und Dekorationen. Sie gehen die Straße hinunter, einer nach dem anderen.

Der erste Festwagen repräsentiert die Sonne. Er hat **gelbe** Verzierungen. Eine Frau in der Mitte trägt ein **weißes** Kleid. Sie sieht aus wie ein Engel. Sie wirft den Leuten **orange**farbene Spielzeuge und Perlen zu.

"Warum wirft sie die Spielsachen und Halsketten?", fragt Frank.

"Für uns!" sagt Hannah, Georges Frau. Hannah hält fünf Halsketten in ihren Händen. Einige Perlen liegen auf dem Boden. Niemand fängt sie. Sie sind schmutzig und **braun**.

Die Parade geht weiter. Es gibt viele Festwagen, und viele Perlen. George und seine Familie rufen: "Wirf etwas her, Meister!" Hannah füllt ihre **schwarze** Tasche mit bunten Spielzeugen und Perlen aus den Festwagen. Frank lernt "Wirf mir etwas zu" zu schreien, um Perlen für sich selbst zu bekommen.

Einer der großen Festwagen hat über 250 Personen. Er ist der größte der Welt.

Schließlich endet die Parade. Die Kinder und die Erwachsenen sind glücklich. Jeder geht nach Hause, Frank ist müde. Er ist außerdem hungrig und will essen. Er folgt George und seiner Familie ins **rote** Haus. Auf dem Tisch steht ein großer, runder Kuchen. Er sieht aus wie ein Ring, mit einem Loch in der Mitte. Auf dem Kuchen befindet sich **lila**, **grüne** und **gelbe** Glasur.

"Das ist Dreikönigskuchen", sagt Hannah. "Wir essen jeden Mardi Gras Dreikönigskuchen."

Hannah schneidet ein Stück Kuchen, sie gibt ein Stück George, ein Stück den Kinder, und ein Stück Frank. Frank probiert den Kuchen. Es ist köstlich! Es schmeckt wie Zimt, es ist weich, aber plötzlich beißt Frank in Plastik.

"Aua!" sagt Frank. Frank hört auf zu essen, er zieht ein Plastikbaby aus dem Kuchen.

"Es gibt noch eine weitere Tradition", sagt George. "Der Kuchen hat ein Baby in sich, die Person, die das Baby bekommt, kauft den nächsten Kuchen."

"Das bin ich!" sagt Frank.

Alle lachen. George lädt Frank zu einer weiteren Parade am **Montag** ein.

Frank geht glücklich nach Hause. Er liebt Mardi Gras.

VOKABELLISTE

Violett	violet
Blau	blue
Farben	colors
Rot	red

Grün	green
Lila	purple
Gold	gold
Freitag	Friaday
Woche	Week
Samstag	Saturday
Sonntag	Sunday
Dienstag	Tuesday
Mittwoch	Wednesday
Donnerstag	Thursday
Gelb	yellow
Weiß	white
Orange	orange
Braun	brown
Schwarz	black
Montag	Monday

FRAGEN

1) Wie würden Sie Franks neues Haus beschreiben?

    a) langweilig

    b) farbenfroh

    c) winzig

    d) einsam

2) Welche Farbe repräsentiert Mardi Gras in New Orleans?

    a) blau

    b) weiß

    c) orange

    d) Gold

3) Mardi Gras ist eine Feier:

a) nur für Erwachsene.

b) aus der Tradition der jüdischen Gemeide.

c) in New Orleans berühmt.

d) die man zu Hause feiert.

4) Was davon ist nicht auf einem Karnevalswagen?

a) Menschen

b) Computer

c) Spielzeug

d) Perlen

5) Was passiert, wenn Sie das Baby in einem Dreikönigskuchen finden?

a) Sie weinen

b) Sie müssen sich um das Baby kümmern

c) geben es Ihrem Freund

d) Sie müssen einen Königskuchen kaufen

ANTWORTEN

1) Wie würden Sie Franks neues Haus beschreiben?

a) langweilig

2) Welche Farbe repräsentiert Mardi Gras in New Orleans?

d) Gold

3) Mardi Gras ist eine Feier:

c) in New Orleans berühmt.

4) Was davon ist nicht auf einem Karnevalswagen?

b) Computer

5) Was passiert, wenn Sie das Baby in einem Dreikönigskuchen finden?

d) Sie müssen einen Dreikönigskuchen kaufen.

Translation of the Story

Mardi Gras

STORY

Frank steps out his front door. His new house is **violet** with **blue** windows. The **colors** are very bright for a house. In New Orleans, his new home, buildings are colorful.

He is new to the neighborhood. Frank does not have any friends yet. The house next to him is a tall, **red** building. A family lives there. Frank stares at the door, and a man opens it. Frank says hello.

"Hello, neighbor!" says George. He waves. Frank walks to the red house.

"Hi, I'm Frank, the new neighbor," says Frank.

"Nice to meet you. My name is George," George says. The men shake hands. George has a string of lights in his hands. The lights are **green**, **purple** and **gold**.

"What are the lights for?" asks Frank.

"You *are* new," laughs George. "It's Mardi Gras, didn't you know? These colors represent the holiday of carnival here in New Orleans."

"Oh, yes," says Frank. Frank does not know about carnival. He also has no friends to make plans with.

"Today is **Friday**," says George. "There is a parade called Endymion. Will you come with me and the family to watch?"

"Yes," Frank says. "Wonderful!"

George puts the lights on the house. Frank helps George. George turns on the lights. The house looks festive.

The family and Frank go to the parade. During Mardi Gras in New Orleans, there are parades every day. The parades during the **week** are small. The parades on the weekend, **Saturday** and **Sunday**, are big, with many floats and people. There is a king of Mardi Gras. His name is Rex.

Mardi Gras means 'Fat **Tuesday'.** In England, it is called Shrove Tuesday. The holiday is Catholic. It is one day before Ash **Wednesday**, the beginning of Lent. Mardi Gras is the celebration before Lent, a serious time. By **Thursday**, the special days are finished. New Orleans is famous for its Mardi Gras. People have parties and wear masks and costumes. In fact, you can only wear a mask in New Orleans on Mardi Gras. The rest of the year it is illegal!

George and his family watch the parade begin with Frank. Frank is surprised. There are many people watching. They stand in the grass. Floats pass the group. Floats are big structures with people and decorations. They go down the street, one by one.

The first float represents the sun. It has **yellow** decorations. A woman in the middle wears a **white** dress. She looks like an angel. She throws **orange** toys and beads to the people.

"Why does she throw the toys and necklaces?" asks Frank.

"For us!" says Hannah, George's wife. Hannah holds five necklaces in her hands. Some beads are on the ground. Nobody catches them. They are dirty and **brown**.

The parade continues. There are many floats, and many beads. George and his family shout, "Throw me something, mister!" Hannah fills her **black** bag with colorful toys and beads from the floats. Frank learns to shout "Throw me something!" to get beads for himself.

One big float has over 250 people on it. It is the largest in the world.

Finally, the parade ends. The children and the adults are happy. Everyone goes home. Frank is tired. He is also hungry and wants to eat. He follows George and his family into the **red** house. There is a big, round cake on the table. It looks like a ring, with a hole in the middle. The cake has **purple**, **green** and **yellow** frosting on top.

"This is king cake," Hannah says. "We eat king cake every Mardi Gras."

Hannah cuts a piece of cake. She gives one piece to George, one piece to the children, and one piece to Frank. Frank tastes the cake. It is delicious! It tastes like cinnamon. It is soft. But suddenly Frank bites into plastic.

"Ouch!" says Frank. Frank stops eating. He pulls a plastic baby out of the cake.

"There is one more tradition," says George. "The cake has a baby in it. The person who gets the baby buys the next cake."

"That's me!" Frank says.

Everyone laughs. George invites Frank to another parade on **Monday.**

Frank goes home happy. He loves Mardi Gras.

CHAPTER 3
Weird Weather / Weather

HANDLUNG

Ivan ist zwölf Jahre alt. Er besucht seine Großeltern am Wochenende. Er liebt es, seine Großeltern zu besuchen. Oma gibt ihm jeden Tag Kekse und Milch. Opa bringt ihm tolle Sachen bei. Dieses Wochenende geht er zu ihnen.

Es ist Februar. Wo Ivan ist, ist es **Winter**. Im Februar **schneit** es gewöhnlich. Ivan liebt den Schnee. Er spielt darin und rollt ihn zu Bällen. Dieses Februarwochenende ist das Wetter anders. Die Sonne scheint; es ist **sonnig** und fast **heiß**! Ivan trägt ein T-Shirt zum Haus seiner Großeltern.

"Hi, Opa! Hi, Oma!" sagt Ivan.

"Hallo, Ivan!" sagt Oma.

"Ivan! Wie geht's dir?" fragt Opa.

"Mir geht es gut", sagt er und umarmt seine Großeltern. Ivan verabschiedet sich von seiner Mutter.

Sie gehen ins Haus. "Dieses Wetter ist seltsam", sagt Oma. "Februar ist immer **kalt** und **wolkig**. Ich verstehe es nicht!"

"Es ist der **Klimawandel**", sagt Ivan. In der Schule lernt Ivan etwas über Umweltverschmutzung und Müll. Das Wetter ändert sich aufgrund von Veränderungen in der **Atmosphäre**. Der Klimawandel ist der Unterschied im Wetter im Laufe der Zeit.

"Ich weiß nichts über den Klimawandel", sagt Opa. "Ich **sage** das Wetter nach dem, was ich sehe **voraus**."

"Was meinst du damit?" fragt Ivan.

"Heute Morgen ist der **Himmel** rot", sagt Opa, "daher weiß ich, dass ein **Sturm** kommt."

"Wie?" fragt Ivan.

"Roter Himmel am Morgen, Seeleute sind gewarnt, roter Himmel in der Nacht, Seemannsfreude", Opa erzählt Ivan von diesem Sprichwort.

Wenn der Himmel bei Sonnenaufgang rot ist, bedeutet das, dass Wasser in der Luft ist. Das Licht der Sonne leuchtet rot. Der Sturm kommt auf dich zu. Wenn der Himmel bei Sonnenuntergang rot ist, geht das schlechte Wetter. Ohne **Wetterexperten** beobachten die Menschen den Himmel nach Hinweisen über das Wetter.

"Wie sagen Wetterexperten das Wetter voraus?", fragt Ivan.

"Sie schauen sich Muster in der Atmosphäre an", sagt Oma. "Sie schauen auf die Temperatur, ob es heiß oder kalt ist. Und sie schauen auf den Luftdruck, was in der Atmosphäre passiert."

"Ich prognostiziere das Wetter anders", sagt Opa. "Ich weiß zum Beispiel, dass es heute **regnen** wird."

"Wie?" fragt Ivan.

"Die Katze", sagt Opa. Ivan sieht die Katze an. Die Katze öffnet den Mund und sagt HATSCHI.

"Wenn die Katze niest oder schnarcht, bedeutet das, dass Regen kommt", sagt Opa. "Es mag **nieseln** oder es mag sehr **regnerisch** sein, aber es wird regnen."

Plötzlich hören sie ein lautes Geräusch. Ivan schaut aus dem Fenster. Regentropfen fallen schwer, der Regen ist laut. Ivan kann nicht hören, was sein Großvater sagt.

"Was?" sagt Ivan.

"Es regnet in Strömen", sagt Opa, lächelnd.

"Ha!" lacht Ivan.

"Ich kenne einen anderen Weg, das Wetter zu sagen", sagt Oma.

Oma beobachtet die Spinnen, um zu sehen, wann das Wetter kalt sein wird. Am Ende des **Sommers** ändert sich das Wetter. Der **Herbst** bringt frische, kühle Luft. Oma weiß, wenn Spinnen reinkommen, bedeutet das, dass kaltes Wetter kommt. Spinnen machen es sich vor dem

Winter drinne gemütlich. So weiß Oma, wann das Winterwetter kommt.

Der Regen hört auf, Großvater und Ivan gehen raus. Opa und Oma leben in einem Haus im Wald. Das Haus hat Bäume um sich herum, es ist ein kleines Haus. Ivan ist kalt in seinem T-Shirt. Das Wetter ist nicht sonnig. Die Luft bewegt sich, es ist **windig**. Der Wind bläst durch Ivans Haar.

"Jetzt ist es **kalt**", sagt Ivan.

"Ja", sagt Opa. "Wie hoch ist die Temperatur?"

"Keine Ahnung", sagt Ivan. "Ich habe kein Thermometer."

"Du brauchst keins", sagt Opa. Großvater sagt Ivan, er soll zuhören. Ivan hört ein Geräusch: Kri-Kri-Kri-Kri. Es ist ein Insekt. Das Kri-Kri-Kri ist der Klang von Grillen, erklärt Großvater Ivan. Ivan zählt das Kri für 14 Sekunden. Großvater fügt 40 zu dieser Zahl hinzu. Das ist die Temperatur draußen. Ivan wusste nicht, Grillen sind wie Thermometer.

Oma kommt aus dem Haus. Sie lächelt, sie sieht Ivan beim Zählen des Grillengeräusches zu. "Zeit für Kekse und Milch!" sagt sie.

"Hurra!" sagt Ivan.

"Oh, schau!" sagt Oma. "Es ist ein Regenbogen." Der Regenbogen geht vom Haus bis zum Wald. Er hat viele Farben: rot, orange, gelb, blau und grün. Der Regenbogen ist wunderschön, Oma, Opa und Ivan schauen sich den regenbogen an. Er verschwindet und sie gehen hinein.

"Kekse und Milch für alle", sagt Oma. Sie gibt Ivan einen warmen Schokoladenkeks.

"Nicht für mich", sagt Opa. "Ich will Tee."

"Warum Tee?" sagt Oma. Sie hält zwei Gläser mit Milch in den Händen.

"Ich **fühle** mich **nicht wohl**", sagt Opa. Er lacht, Ivan und Oma lachen mit ihm.

VOKABELLISTE

Winter	winter
schneien	to snow
Wetter	weather
sonnig	sunny
heiß	hot
kalt	cold
wolkig	cloudy

Klimawandel	climate change
Atmosphäre	atmosphere
voraussagen	predict
Himmel	sky
Sturm	storm
Wetterexperten	weathermen
nieseln	drizzle
regnerisch	rainy
In Strömen regnen	raining cats and dogs
Sommer	summer
Herbst	autumn
windig	windy
Temperatur	temperature
Thermometer	thermometer
Regenbogen	rainbow
nicht wohlfühlen	under the weather

FRAGEN

1) Wie ist das Wetter im Februar normalerweise?

    a) heiß

    b) kalt

    c) sonnig

    d) frisch

2) Woher weiß Opa, wie das Wetter sein wird?

    a) er sieht Fernsehen

    b) Wetterexperten

    c) er beobachtet die Natur

    d) er sagt das Wetter vorraus

3) Was bedeutet es, in Strömen zu regnen?

    a) es regnet Ströme

b) es regnet nur ein wenig

c) Flüsse fließen schneller

d) es regnet sehr stark

4) Was bedeutet es, wenn Spinnen reinkommen?

a) sie sind hungrig

b) sie sind bereit, Eier zu legen

c) Kälte kommt auf uns zu

d) warmes Wetter kommt

5) Warum bittet Opa um Tee statt Milch?

a) er fühlt sich etwas krank

b) er ist allergisch gegen Milch

c) er will ein heißes Getränk

d) um Oma wütend zu machen

ANTWORTEN

1) Wie ist das Wetter im Februar normalerweise?

    b) kalt

2) Woher weiß Opa, wie das Wetter sein wird?

    d) er sagt das Wetter vorraus

3) Was bedeutet es, in Strömen zu regnen?

    d) es regnet sehr stark

4) Was bedeutet es, wenn Spinnen reinkommen?

    c) Kälte kommt auf uns zu

5) Warum bittet Opa um Tee statt Milch?

    a) er fühlt sich etwas krank

Translation of the Story

Weird Weather

STORY

Ivan is twelve years old. He visits his grandparents on the weekend. He loves to visit his grandparents. Grandma gives him cookies and milk every day. Grandpa teaches him neat things. This weekend he goes to their house.

It is February. Where Ivan is, it is **winter**. In February, it usually **snows**. Ivan loves the snow. He plays in it and rolls it into balls. This February weekend, the **weather** is different. The sun is shining; it is **sunny** and almost **hot**! Ivan wears a T-shirt to his grandparent's house.

"Hi, Grandpa! Hi, Grandma!" Ivan says.

"Hello, Ivan!" Grandma says.

"Ivan! How are you?" says Grandpa.

"I'm good," he says, and he hugs his grandparents. Ivan says goodbye to his mom.

They go into the house. "This weather is strange," says Grandma. "February is always **cold** and **cloudy**. I don't understand!"

"It is **climate change**," says Ivan. In school, Ivan learns about contamination and pollution. The weather changes because of changes in the **atmosphere**. Climate change is the difference in the weather over time.

"I don't know about climate change," says Grandpa. "I **predict** the weather by what I see."

"What do you mean?" asks Ivan.

"This morning, the **sky** is red," says Grandpa. "This means I know a **storm** is coming."

"How?" asks Ivan.

"Red sky in the morning, sailors take warning. Red sky at night, sailor's delight." Grandpa tells Ivan about this saying.

If the sky is red at sunrise, it means there is water in the air. The light of the sun shines red. The storm is coming towards you. If the sky is red at sunset, the bad weather is leaving. Without **weathermen**, people watch the sky for clues about the weather.

"How do weathermen predict the weather?" asks Ivan.

"They look at patterns in the atmosphere," says Grandma. "They look at temperature, if it is hot or cold. And they look at air pressure, what is happening in the atmosphere."

"I predict the weather differently," says Grandpa. "For example, I know today it will **rain**."

"How?" asks Ivan.

"The cat," says Grandpa. Ivan looks at the cat. The cat opens its mouth and says 'ah-CHOO'.

"When the cat sneezes or snores, that means rain is coming," says Grandpa. It may **drizzle** or it may be very **rainy**, but it will rain."

Suddenly, they hear a loud sound. Ivan looks out the window. Drops of rain are falling hard. The rain is loud. Ivan can't hear what his Grandpa says.

"What?" says Ivan.

"It's **raining cats and dogs,**" says Grandpa, smiling.

"Ha!" laughs Ivan.

"I know another way to tell the weather," says Grandma.

Grandma watches the spiders to see when the weather will be cold. At the end of **summer**, the weather changes. **Autumn** brings fresh, cool air. Grandma knows that when spiders come inside, it means cold weather is coming. The spiders make a house inside before winter. That is how grandma knows when the winter weather comes.

The rain stops. Grandpa and Ivan go out. Grandpa and Grandma live in a house in the forest. The house has trees around it. It is a small house. Ivan is cold in his T-shirt. The weather is not sunny. The air is moving. It is **windy**. The wind blows through Ivan's hair.

"It is **cold** now," says Ivan.

"Yes," says Grandpa. "What is the temperature?"

"I don't know," says Ivan. "I don't have a thermometer."

"You don't need one," says Grandpa. Grandpa tells Ivan to listen. Ivan hears a sound: *cri-cri-cri*. It is an insect. The *cri-cri-cri* is the sound of crickets. Grandpa teaches Ivan. Ivan counts the *cri* for fourteen seconds. Grandpa adds 40 to that number. That is the temperature outside. Ivan did not know crickets were like thermometers.

Grandma comes out of the house. She smiles. She watches Ivan counting the *cri* sound. "Time for cookies and milk!" she says.

"Yay!" says Ivan.

"Oh, look!" says Grandma. "It's a rainbow." The rainbow goes from the house to the forest. It has many colors: red, orange, yellow, blue and green. The rainbow is beautiful. Grandma, Grandpa and Ivan watch the rainbow. It disappears and they go inside.

"Cookies and milk for everyone," says Grandma. She gives Ivan a warm chocolate cookie.

"Not for me," says Grandpa. "I want tea."

"Why tea?" says Grandma. She has two milks in her hand.

"I'm feeling **under the weather**," says Grandpa. He laughs. Ivan and Grandma laugh with him.

CONCLUSION

You did it!

You finished a whole book in a brand new language. That in and of itself is quite the accomplishment, isn't it?

Congratulate yourself on time well spent and a job well done. Now that you've finished the book, you have familiarized yourself with over 500 new vocabulary words, comprehended the heart of 3 short stories, and listened to loads of dialogue unfold, all without going anywhere!

Charlemagne said "To have another language is to possess a second soul." After immersing yourself in this book, you are broadening your horizons and opening a whole new path for yourself.

Have you thought about how much you know now that you did not know before? You've learned everything from how to greet and how to express your emotions to basics like colors and place words. You can tell time and ask question. All without opening a schoolbook. Instead, you've cruised through fun, interesting stories and possibly listened to them as well.

Perhaps before you weren't able to distinguish meaning when you listened to German. If you used the audiobook, we bet you can now pick out meanings and words when you hear someone speaking. Regardless, we are sure you have taken an important step to being more fluent. You are well on your way!

Best of all, you have made the essential step of distinguishing in your mind the idea that most often hinders people studying a new language. By approaching German through our short stories and dialogs, instead of formal lessons with just grammar and vocabulary, you are no longer in the 'learning' mindset. Your approach is much more similar to an osmosis, focused on speaking and using the language, which is the end goal, after all!

So, what's next?

This is just the first of five books, all packed full of short stories and dialogs, covering essential, everyday German that will ensure you master the basics. You can find the rest of the books in the series, as well as a whole host of other resources, at LearnLikeNatives.com. Simply add the book to your library to take the next step in your language learning journey. If you are ever in need of new ideas or direction, refer to our 'Speak Like a Native' eBook, available to you for free at LearnLikeNatives.com, which clearly outlines practical steps you can take to continue learning any language you choose.

We also encourage you to get out into the real world and practice your German. You have a leg up on most beginners, after all—instead of pure textbook learning, you have been absorbing the sound and soul of the language. Do not underestimate the foundation you have built reviewing the chapters of this book. Remember, no one feels 100% confident when they speak with a native speaker in another language.

One of the coolest things about being human is connecting with others. Communicating with someone in their own language is a wonderful gift. Knowing the language turns you into a local and opens up your world. You will see the reward of learning languages for many years to come, so keep that practice up!. Don't let your fears stop you from taking the chance to use your German.

Just give it a try, and remember that you will make mistakes. However, these mistakes will teach you so much, so view every single one as a small victory! Learning is growth.

Don't let the quest for learning end here! There is so much you can do to continue the learning process in an organic way, like you did with this book. Add another book from Learn Like a Native to your library. Listen to German talk radio. Watch some of the great German Musical. Put on the latest CD from Sarah Connor. Take cooking lessons in German. Whatever you do, don't stop because every little step you take counts towards learning a new language, culture, and way of communicating.

www.LearnLikeNatives.com

Learn Like a Native is a revolutionary **language education brand** that is taking the linguistic world by storm. Forget boring grammar books that never get you anywhere, Learn Like a Native teaches you languages in a fast and fun way that actually works!

As an international, multichannel, language learning platform, we provide **books, audio guides and eBooks** so that you can acquire the knowledge you need, swiftly and easily.

Our **subject-based learning**, structured around real-world scenarios, builds your conversational muscle and ensures you learn the content most relevant to your requirements. Discover our tools at ***LearnLikeNatives.com***.

When it comes to learning languages, we've got you covered!